How to Beat Your Kids

Without Leaving a Mark

By: Liz M. Mendoza

Order this book online at www.trafford.com
or email orders@trafford.com

Most Trafford titles are also available at major online book retailers.

Printed in the United States of America.

ISBN: 978-1-4269-3924-2 (soft)
ISBN: 978-1-4269-3925-9 (hard)
ISBN: 978-1-4269-3926-6 (ebook)

Library of Congress Control Number: 2010911126

*Our mission is to efficiently provide the world's finest, most comprehensive book publishing
service, enabling every author to experience success. To find out how to publish your
book, your way, and have it available worldwide, visit us online at www.trafford.com*

Trafford rev. 7/28/2010

 www.trafford.com

North America & international
toll-free: 1 888 232 4444 (USA & Canada)
phone: 250 383 6864 ♦ fax: 812 355 4082

(Author's Words)

Sometimes we just have to go all out to make a point. Nothing and no one is ever perfectly made. Life is what it is… just four simple letters and one simply dramatic thing. Why judge one another when we're all trying to figure it out, and heck yes I have one long ass list of questions for GOD because I feel very yipped on this term. Can you really blame me for speaking out the truth? A friend once said just do it; and so Dean my closest, dearest, and truest friend this one's for you. Kids SUCK! I personally do not recommend them.

Table of Contents

Chapter One

Born for this book

It all started when I was nineteen and a half. I was walking down the street thinking inside my head, what's the point of life. I questioned God a trillion questions as I got to the park bench and stared at people passing by. Questions such as "Is it a girl or is it a boy, why am I so hungry, and why the heck did I allow myself to get pregnant by this asshole boyfriend of mine?" How convenient it is to search for answers after you mess up isn't it? What I want to know is "what's the point of it all?" I mean really we take a lifetime to figure out that being young really is the worst part of growing up because we find out later on that we only make stupid mistakes and we're not as bright as we seem to think we are. Suddenly you wake up at age forty and guess what? Oh my god I hate kids!

But I got something to tell you about how to beat your kids without leaving a mark, so listen on good. Remember a time very long ago when you were told "you can't do that" and " mommy knows best" and rest assure when back in the day we didn't need to get smacked because one stern look from across the table and we just knew we were in trouble. Awe the good ole days, god I miss them. I've learned to respect the times when being poor and having nothing much meant I had more than enough and playing with simple marbles or a paddle ball was the best of times. Kids nowadays don't know shit. They couldn't change a flat on a bicycle for the life of them. They don't even know how much fun spinning a top really is. So how do you get back at your kids, well let me take you through my own experience with little ingrate, "I'm glad you stared at walls for hours."

It starts out since they're born you know. Yeah that cute button nose blue eyed wrinkled five pound seven ounce trouble I brought into this world. I knew it then exhausted in that hospital room that he was no angel and the battle was yet to begin. No, it wasn't in the hospital while were there a few days, there he was silent and beautiful. My little monster waited until I went back home and gave me nights; oh god the horrible nights of lack of slept deprivation, I rocked I walked I talked I cursed hell yeah I cursed well until my mother got scared that I'd strangle the little fucker and took him from me. "Excuse me doctor, what do you mean colicky?" "Are you fucking kidding me I got a crier?" As if life hadn't already sucked, go figure, this is why people who can't handle crying kill there own because although I don't agree with them man I know it takes patience to learn to beat your kids right.

First step to beating him quietly and I recommend this to all mothers, rock him for a while and thank god for pacifiers keep twenty if necessary close by. "Awe there my sweet angel rock, rock, rock, suck, suck, suck, smell my sweat off my shirt and yeah very slowly because if you get up too quick he knows you just tried to let him go; that little fucker just knows departure so take it easy like a robber on the prowl, and creep slowly to your bed not the crib itself because your stench is in your bed not the crib and remove your shirt all together with him holing on to it for dear life, so he believes you're still there with him, yeah men are such babies they can't let go since long before they could speak, god forbid you mention it they get so upset. There you have it I beat him for the first time and he didn't feel it because I'm just that good. For the record for those of you who don't believe in the shirt trick trust me it really works at least for me it did I don't know why I fought it so long. It's the best beating you can give a baby, and battle one is now won conquered and shut down. That's right I felt like jumping in the air feet off the ground but I couldn't because one sudden wrong movement and my little devil would wake up and I was not about to fight another hour of him. If I told you it was easy I'd be lying kids just know how to wear you down and trust me they're born with it in them to ruin your life; they don't even have to try. It's like a disease that they carry and we are always in fear for life.

You have to think strategically because there's always something like the harassing little trouble making brat that embarrasses you while shopping in the supermarket "Ma!, Ma! Please buy me this, please!" Then a cry, and a kick, and when all else fails panting all over the floor where people behind you watch your stinking brat like in amazement that you haven't smacked the shit out of that animal, so you pick him up looking at the people in line like "I'm embarrassed, so sorry!" While you're actually pinching his under arm as he gets up letting him know who is the boss and when he yells out you pick him up and whisper wait till we get home, that's right I believe in discipline. The bible states be stern with the rod, and I am old school; it's not abuse to discipline a brat it's called parenting; remember the good old soap in the mouth

4

days; god I wish we could go back to that. Unfortunately my child grew up in the days we can't hit a child isn't that such bullshit; we make these little fuckers and people believe they have the right to tell you how to be a parent. What about when your child believes he's got the right to hit you when he's upset; "no freaken way am I allowing that to happen" One time, one mistake and bang! He knows he's wrong. Heck who needs me to straighten their kid out? Time out has nothing on me.

My favorite life's lesson is called the wall; man who ever invented it is a god in my eyes; there is nothing worse than a two year old that's right two, the evil two's exist; having to sit at the kitchen table facing the wall without moving at all; does it happen hell yes it does; I place him there for punishment to think of what he did wrong and I wash the dishes or something and every five minutes ask him "Do you know what you did wrong? No, okay another five minutes" I wait and straighten him forceful enough to show him I'm not playing; that's right, call me Sergeant Mendoza shit! Now I repeat myself until he finally tells me what he did wrong on his own and I say "why were you wrong?" until he recognizes why he was wrong on his own; walls you got to love them I tell you. Then I say "you're not going to do that again right? Okay you can get down" That's right strategic moves work well, and for the record, my mom used to beat me with belts, brooms, her long ass nails so a wall isn't shit; really? Plus my mom smacked her kids in public for humiliation affect; God bless that! The wall went on until he was about six, because this litter fucker was hardheaded like me; he eventually fell over off the chair because the sittings got longer by minutes and he would just get bored and fall asleep; so I gave it to him and just started sending him to his room, where now I had a door to shut closed and he hated it; so did I because I wasn't sure if he was playing or in bed on punishment. That also gets longer until him or I didn't care anymore, sometimes a spanking on his bosom with a belt; it depended on the gravity of his actions. Truth be told a mother hates spanking her child it's like inflicting pain on oneself; truly but it's necessary at times because discipline is a crucial part of teaching right from wrong I mean how else do we make a good man out of our son.

The concept of beating your kids without leaving a mark sounds like a contradiction in itself and it is; you leave a mark but the mark you eventually leave is them thinking "Damn don't fuck with mom; cause she's a crazy bitch and I love her so much." "Awe isn't that sweet my boy finally a man." I give props to all single mothers; no one knows how hard the task is of raising a child that's born to have issues. It's bad enough I only had one and my son resented me throughout his entire life for ruining his picture perfect family because kids are sheltered until a certain time of their life when they can be spoken to like adults, but by then they do everything in their power to remind you it's all your fault. Why one you may wonder; "hell no was I going to reproduce more shit I always knew one was enough; actually I'd have been fine with not having any; I sacrificed many a things to help him stay sane." An only child isn't a good idea though because I think they tend to go through depressions because of loneliness, a parent isn't a friend or brother; I know this and I can't take away every pain although I really tried hard. "Damn, I'm exhausted; hell living alone now feels so damn good I think it's invigorating" because children drain you they really, really do. They drain you mentally, emotionally, physically, and most of all financially. I mean what happened to the days when no really meant no. It's like I was making up for the shit I never got; I'm pathetic because I caved in much too quick and that's how they become ingrates.

Children in this day and age don't understand sacrifice and why my son doesn't understand why I had two jobs most of my life is shocking to me. I have won though in the long run because being a mom means never giving away your place, and if that means war with the losers of the world (<u>We'll see this chapter later on</u>) until death do me part, then by gosh I will win in the end. Why is it that I can't understand how a high school teacher; which by the way are not like when I was in school. When I was in school teachers wore plaid long skirts with long thick socks underneath and black shiny shoes; there wasn't this new age twenty one year old looking broad with cleavage all out. How is it possible that this new age teacher can have the audacity to tell me on parent teacher night that kids have so much stress; "Are you kidding me with this cracker-jack education?" Isn't bad enough we struggle making our children come out sane, and good, but now we have to deal with tootsies bullshit evaluation in front of my kid. What are they just stupid now? What ever happened to when we had to use encyclopedias? Or lived in the library? "Now kids just want to cut and paste straight out of the internet; where is their brain?" Thanks a lot teachers you've just earned a "congratulations on being a dumb ass position that's so replaceable; no one respects you; you're just a title" for "no one important, and that's why kids don't respect you."

I remember the first time I took my son to school. I walked him to the doors of the school entrance where I'd hand him off to his line of other demon children. I cried; yes call me foolish but it was the beginning of him growing away from me; at least that's what it felt like. I didn't know that I'd be happy to be set free, today. I beat my kid and dang it; it was my job as a good mother. Teachers blame parents but most of the children's life is in school; years ago parents didn't help children with what they knew half of; it was up to the school to use the time allotted to making sure kids came out winners at end. Do you beat your kid and not leave a mark; well technically we're all marked just differently; old school is good school. I spent most of his first day of school sort of disoriented my mind so concerned; it's part of motherhood a constant worry for your kids. It ends well then and you've just exhausted yourself once more because you had this child. School years was no joke either, from writing his name reluctantly; I mean maybe I'm nuts but I loved school; maybe being poor and having nothing makes one look forward to possibility; I don't know but my son hated it all the way through it was the task of all tasks when he couldn't figure it out and for most of elementary years he did pretty good. The teachers always complained of his disruption and talking too much and missing homework, I'm sorry I was busy working two jobs and having such little time for this part of his life I was busy supporting myself and my child, so screw you teachers saying he talks to much; maybe he needed to talk because he was mostly alone; motherhood is never perfect neither is being a child; I get it.

I say born for this book because he made possible what I write. Don't you just love the lesson of life; from baby to kid, to teenager, to adult and me well I'm now at old? Having done all that I've done to beat my child without leaving a mark has given me grays and a lot to take in and what's remarkable is that I am glad I was part of it, but really don't ever have kids; I don't suggest them. The word (mother) such a huge thing; and we are unappreciated for what's most of our life, (ain't) that some shit. Yeah I said (ain't) I have the right to write like I please because if kids can spell (iight) to mean alright then I can say (ain't)! Have you noticed the mouths on children today or even the skinny jean usage unless the pants fall off their ass, and can you believe that dress codes don't exist; I say go back to uniform style because some of the kids I've seen in my day and age are horrifying and even disgusting or trampy at that. Thank god for my character my son never wore his pants off his ass maybe a bit baggy and I really mean a bit; I don't play that shit with rights in my home; "I made you I had you"; and that's how it goes. Plus I was a smart mother I bought his clothes and made sure he showed them to me out of the dressing room; no strikes with me; again I like to win; he couldn't have me beat unless he started working and bring in his own; I basically bought his clothes until he left home, (A plus) for me.

I remember Junior high school and the transition to moving to a bigger school. But before that his graduation from fifth grade; isn't that a priceless moment you stand there in tears wishing that maybe his father could have seen him so proud and nervous all the while thinking that's my little boy all grown up; but hey how did this happen life passed by my very own eyes; and I wasn't just a woman; I was a package deal me and my young boy together in this world and nothing and no one can tear us apart. I was so proud of him and also proud of me; I felt so grown up; that little fucker was born to break my little heart; who knew; who knew you could love this little devil more than yourself. Awe kids; I hate them. Don't you?

Chapter Two
Four Christmas's

My son's four Christmas's and I only say four because the first and second year of life he can't remember correctly or even feel to have enjoyed. But I did for him; I'm such a huge kid; maybe it's because I never got what I wanted being one out of five and neglected. After he turned six; I stopped celebrating such a fake child holiday; I hate Santa where was he in my younger years. When my son tore off the paper from his huge purple (Barney) that big dumb dinosaur; what was he anyway; if not so stupidly annoying; but he had to have it whenever I asked "what would you like Santa to get you for Christmas?" He'd start singing "I love you, you love me…" The crock of shit we feed our kids, to then scare the living shit out of them when we take them to see Barney at the mall. They don't comprehend television yet and Barney's apparently too huge in turn scary, maybe they should use midgets for those types of costumes, "I wonder?" That's another thing about trying to beat your kids without leaving a mark because you're the one who ends up with the scars; God forbid you forget Barney. Can you imagine the long joy ride from Hartford Connecticut in which you don't like to stop until you get back home; and after a while your child realizes Barney is no where to be found and starts whaling and begging for you to get Barney; that dumb purple Christmas headache bites you in the ass once more; damn it! So you try soothing your three to four year old child with his "I love you" bullshit hit song. I want to know where the heck I signed up for this because I feel like I'm under contract. Yeah my son has me on locked down, and frankly how many years are left; this is prison yup! Motherhood is jail. Until suddenly silence and you remember he can't last awake in the car for more than a half hour; that's right I used to drive him at night when he couldn't sleep as a baby; yeah I got some tricks alright. Score!

It wasn't only Barney; what about Power Rangers sure it's a great idea to mesmerize kids with fighting; I prefer to call it self defense personally, besides I never let him play with toy guns; he might have turned on me like "Here Ma; thanks for the rules that sucked!" Toy Story; now that was GREAT! Yeah because I used it to show him how the boy was so bad and no one liked him; score again mommy! Yeah I pat myself on my back; like "that's right you learned that because of me." It's funny how he had a Power Ranger room; for more than he really should have it's like he was about fourteen before we actually changed the look of his room to look like a teenager's room. They really want to grow up; yet love being a kid. He slept with his plush dog in his arms that some chick gave him until he left home at nineteen. I used to look at him sleeping and even though he pissed me off through the years in many ways and many times; the mind plays tricks on you and all you see is your baby sleeping safely. Yeah I definitely want no more kids; I never want to go through that again; dang; it's like I paid the price for having sex. This should be what the schools should publish on bulletin; SEX EQUALS LIFETIME OF HEADACHE TO ALL FEMALES!!! Or MOTHERHOOD SUCKS GIRLS!!! Or DO YOU REALLY WANT TO BE YOUR MOTHER GIRL??? The perfect eye openers; or maybe they can invite me over for an hour; oh they'll hate kids trust me. I remember the days oh the beautiful days when a girl disappeared from school and you wondered why she never came back that year; it's because schools didn't promote pregnant girls as cool.

Christmas number two; wow my first real Christmas tree. I didn't have a tree I had gifts under the bed when we all woke up Santa didn't step in Ghetto neighborhoods, so I knew of this fake holiday at a very young age. A train set I went and purchased, and man when that train went in circles me and my boy so amazed; I felt like a kid and he felt so big; the two of us wondering which was our present because I had a roommate; so I was now a big kid being treated like I had never been as a child except I was an adult learning life through my friend who was fifteen years older than me and teaching me responsibility for the sake of my child. She scorned both of us constantly only my son was mine. I was so excited and so was my son ripping off paper together and here we both always got what we wanted; we both made a list and got everything on it; man I loved that. To be struggling and still make dreams come true. As my son got older I used every one of his presents as collateral; the price of being a kid. Screw up and garbage meets toy; except he grew up and realized I would take it from the garbage and hide things in my closet. Eventually it became throwing cell phones hard to the floor damaging them; but like a sucker that we become I basically gave myself more reasons for spending because I was angry with him and now I paid the price financially; oh and for the record making your child watch you place his three hundred dollar cell phone into a of glass full of water is a priceless moment. "Master card got nothing on me" What a rush that still gives me. Yeah I bought it; and had to buy him another out of needing to have communication with him because teenagers love miscommunication I learned. But the fact that I was still Sergeant Mendoza when he was shocked by my way or no way attitude was and has always made me proud of my self; score baby score! AAAHHH!!!!!! I can actually hear the cheering for me. "Cause and affect" I say; you cause me to anger and the affect is so unexpected I leave you shocked and shaken. I'm not the barking annoying Chihuahua I'm down right the mean fucken wolf. My son has heard my bark and let me tell you; even his friends have heard a piece of me; that's right call me THE BITCH because I am when needed; I'm trying to raise a good man and nothing and no one will stop my fight; NO ONE!

Christmas number three hey who said I wanted bird with my Christmas tree? Christmas number three was an oozy. Yikes! I don't mean to be about me but hey when a bird flies out of the fucken Christmas tree that I'm feeding water to; hell fucken yeah everyone is on there own and my room is the fucken barrier between me and the bird. Sorry son but I got there first. My roommate caught the flying fuck with a pillow case my son by her leg and set it free outside; lectured me about what a fucked up mom I was but hey for the record my son was by my room if he wasn't fast enough then that's too bad everyone for themselves; giggle. That's right tooth and bone till death do us part but flying animals changes everything. It was a good Christmas his sixed birthday Christmas well that was until Jack ass dad decided he wanted finally to be part of my sons life and not only wasn't he man enough to come on his own he used his brother to convince me to talk with him; so naturally I wanted my son to view his dad as a good man; what a fucken asshole. I should have slapped that motherfucker; I should have spit in his face for the disrespect of him telling me if I didn't love him then he wouldn't love my son; I should have kicked his ass and then showed my son what a loser he was; but no I was a good woman and made him look like a super star to my child and all I got out of this fucken Christmas was a mother fucker telling my son on his every other weekend visits that we were apart because I didn't want to be with him; go figure you do something right for someone to blame you for ruining your sons life; hence why he's always blamed me for ruining his life. For the record we should have the right as mothers to shoot the fucker who ruins a kid's brain, at least in the state of New York; I say, really. It isn't fair the place of being a mom; it seems we're the blame for everything and then to top it off your roommate blames you for allowing the kids father in your life so it's always your fault no matter where you turn for advice; hum! I have got to warn people that it's not a good idea and kids should really accept daddy sucks. Let your child spend a lifetime of hate for dad for once so you can shine like the star that you truly are; what a great idea I wish I thought of that years ago instead of feeling guilty that my son wasn't raised by mom and loser dad.

Then that's when you decide Christmas SUCKS! Then and there after you evaluate, do we really need a holiday to have to deal with assholes like my sons father who used this specific holiday to get to my son; hell no! I will not let him do that. My son doesn't seem to understand that I spent basically nineteen years of my entire forty year life trying to protect his ass from the idiots that could harm him and all I got was late nights of lack of sleep, worries that he was in harm, dealing with it's okay to masturbate son, to it's not okay to hide a girl in your closet; and oh yeah the best one of all; oh okay you made your point by running away but what was the plan? Yes he always tried to beat me but I was still smarter and wiser; it's like two kids fighting with one another but one is always stronger. Well that's because my life taught me well the hard way since I've been on my own since I was fifteen. All he knows is "Mom can you please pop this pimple it hurts." Yes I wallow in glory and I really should because I beat my kid without leaving a mark, the only mark left after he left is that he misses the heck out of me, as he should so fuck all those who talk shit, Sergeant Mendoza conquered and did what she did for the sake of her kid; not every parent can say that so proudly so all you talking loser moms FUCK YOU and your comments! You don't even know what it is to struggle with your son on your own! Walk my shoes and you'll only stumble because frankly all you are is a weak whiny complainer with excuses.

Yeah I so love hating Christmas, don't you? All it did was teach my son things he needed not know and me that I don't have to tolerate bullshit from no one just because they were once and I really mean past tense part of my life. I wish women could be allowed to shoot their ex's in the fucken head and relieve ourselves of such disgust; wouldn't that be a good fucken Christmas. "Dear Santa all I want for Christmas is a magnum 44, with fifteen rounds loaded so I can empty the fucken thing on a man who once got me pregnant and won't leave me alone; PS. Deliver it before Christmas so I can use it that specific day; thanks! I owe you one Liz." Wouldn't that be great ladies; I know you feel the same just admit it; it's okay to feel that way; I understand. "Shout, shout let it all out these are the things that we dream about, c'mon I'm talking to you c'mon!" Sometimes people know the right words don't you think? As far as Christmas goes it's the worst holiday in my book I don't care if Santa falls from the fucken sky he still owes me a fucken explanation for being so fat damn it! If I traveled the world on one single night you bet your ass I'd be thin; I'd be so thin I'd look like a cigarette and smoke myself into nothing. The only good gift I ever got from some fake ass Santa was the oversized teddy bear my mothers lover Mr. T gave me one Christmas because he felt guilt that I saw him fucking her doggy style right before the holidays, so to my surprise he gave me the best present in our house of kids; I spent many of nights hugging my dearest teddy bear until my stupid little sister; killed my bear one Christmas when she got a doctors set for Christmas.

I think back now and realize man Christmas really sucks and why do we do it to our children; we lie and say if you're a good boy Santa will give you all that you want; what a crock of shit man; let's be for real, really? Santa won't bring me a fucken vibrator; I'd have to buy that shit all on my own; and will he really bring me Mr. Wonderful; hell to the fucken no! Let's get realistic; he's a buffoon; some sloppy character made up since long ago way before my time, you know what I want I want his fucken boots; that's right I want to walk around naked wearing his rubber boots, and celebrate Christmas saying "Hello fucken Christmas come get with this!" Then spend the day naked without any kids; now that's a fucken holiday, ladies. I got you, trust me; I'm saying it all for the mothers; it's like if when you become mother, there's nothing else to you; and that's bullshit; they should warn us at childhood because this sucks to shit! Four fucken

Christmas's and you know what, that was enough! A lifetime of wanting to make right a holiday that truly sucks.

I'd like to go on record for a moment... You get pregnant and people are like "awe, soon you'll be a mommy and realize it the best thing." "BULLSHIT!" It's giving up the fun cool stiff like smoking a joint, or partying till morning; and hanging alone cause "fucken (A) I need privacy!" It's giving up having sex like an animal because children can hear; it's giving up being able to walk naked just because I feel horny as shit! It's life being sucked out of you slowly so that you can care of no one more than your kid; and what happened to the moments when it was about adventure; god forbid you speak out loud and say "Dang, I need a good fucking on the wall or the floor." I mean really; how to beat your kids without leaving a mark? How about I write that I'm freaking locked down because I had a child; not that it doesn't have its moments some wonderful tears but man it's a fucken prison; who the hell was it that recommended it; I want to beat the shit out of them. "I love you son; but man my life could have and would have been different." It's nothing personal but no one ever sees through the eyes of the moms; but I do because I have and even though children seem beautiful; they can also be an ugly thing; first it starts out with a colicky child and then you're stuck with "Why did I choose to have children?"

Yeah that's the truth; and he'll probably leave me in an old folks home as soon as he can; "So, why does adoption sound so bad; really we should vote for giving someone else our headache before it becomes one." I used to dream of the good times; the laughter and all the ways I could get laid; now I've just become an old lady because it's how children make you feel after a lifetime of caring whether or not they are safe; point to be taken is "Unless you hate Christmas we're not on the same page. Or maybe you're not a mother, and if your not, god bless you! I celebrated one Christmas too many, can you tell?"

Chapter Three

LEARNING AND TEACHING

The thing about learning and teaching a child what we have learned; is somewhat a dilemma; I mean we can't just teach them everything we've done. "(Ain't) that's right I said it, some shit!" We suddenly become the one person who has to by force say, "no, no don't touch." when we all have been there. "No, drugs are no good:" what happened to those great moments; I lost track of time because somewhere along the way it became un-cool if your child ever imagined you high. "Can you believe that as a mother we want to be un-cool? I mean what?" We sacrifice every thing about us; man it blows and for what to be someone's mother; "if I could reverse time; I'd go back to not having sex, yeah those were the good times and nothing so complicated was part of me. "My child now man seems to think I have no coolness, or that I'm dumb as a stump because I am the negative force that drives that little fuck." He should be hailing me and thanking me as much because I am the one who taught him every thing including throwing a football; "how cool is that?" "STOP THE CHILD PROCESS, PLEASE DEAR GOD!" His first bike ride was me holding the back of his seat and pretending he rode well until his confidence peaked. "I AM GODESS Mendoza" if you ask me.

There was a time when a mere fall to the ground brought my child to me whaling and leaving me to kiss his damn hand saying" It's okay now mommy kissed it." "Fucken (A) I am great!" I remember the first time my son ever fell, I was walking the streets in Connecticut with my brother and cousin; and picture this a cold winter windy day where garbage on the ground lifts and flies by, but there my son in the stroller and I stop and turn around away from the wind to light up that good old fashion Newport cigarette, "AH!" and my stroller moves into the curb tilting with my son in it, and my heart just stops and

I scream and cry hysterically where my brother picks up the stroller and the baby's strapped well in the blankets not feeling the hit because I packed him so well and my brother holding me and the baby saying "He's okay." Even a cigarette I couldn't enjoy, "FUCK!" When does it end? Moms can't possibly have a sense of humor, can they? "That almost pushed me to stop smoking screw that I want my liberties too;" are children that evil? "I'm thinking so."

I once rammed a girl against the railing of my stairs; "yeah I'm a bully when you mess with what's mine." You teach your son he cannot hit girls and all of a sudden some little bitch from upstairs wants to abuse my little boy. "GO TELL YOUR MOTHER: I'LL KICK HER ASS, TOO!!!" Yeah I was a mean protector. Her mother never spoke to me again but I didn't care; I warned her a few times about her daughter and obviously she didn't get the point across to her little brat so "I just took it upon me because I gave a shit." We teach our kids the opposite of what we truly are "(ain't) that some shit!" If my son were anything like me I'd be in a lot worse situation "thank God, he's the quiet one in our special twisted relationship." "He hates me I hate him; he loves me to sickness and I love him to death." When you have children you realize you're in a lousy marriage that you can never remove yourself away from 'cause it's for fucken ever.

"Do you know how many times one has to say "don't touch?" before a child gets it; or "don't speak" or "STOP!" it (ain't) easy I tell you. How many dishes does a child have to break before he learns how to wash the plate right? How many glasses break before you learn to buy plastic cups? How many times must a mother check if her son wiped his ass right? "Yeah motherhood means ladies… hosing that little nasty ass in the shower because it's so nasty you want to throw up." Are you getting the picture about teaching and learning, now? Oh we teach but also we learn. You would not believe the countless memories I have to live with of my sons crap (literal). They forget all this when they're in high school and think their shit don't smell. "WHY?" Because mommy's not cool remember. Four Christmas's and all that crap and still we get no respect because we apparently have to wait for them to truly grow up; where was I when they passed out these instructions. It would have made my final decision on abortion, really. As if that isn't enough?

Remember back in the day when you'd take the bottle and fill it quarter ways up with milk, then baby food veggie and baby food fruit with a touch of powdered rice cereal because it was just him never being un-content afterwards and you were just lazy with this angry little brat. "Why is it babies make it difficult for you to feed them with a spoon?" Contemplate that for a minute. How many children do you see ever really clean "those sloppy little punks can find ways to embarrass you can't they?" Guess what though I was lucky because my little fucker was a neat child and hated to get dirty and still he is that way today. He was made for military life if you ask me. I mean "who folds their underwear at age five into cute organized squares without being told and curls up their socks into round balls or folds shirts and puts them away in the drawer by color or type" my son that's who. Even on his sloppiest days his room is so organize and his closet is nothing like mine. I once told him to clean his room as a child and that kid organized it like a fucken home decorator and ever since then has never changed.

I learned that I have a neat freak; and taught him a bit to let lose. We basically learned with each other how a team is supposed to work. It hasn't been easy and it's never really over. We have fights with each other because a kid is like a husband only you keep the power at all times, and even when and if you're wrong you get to say "I'm sorry" and walk away making him smile. As my son started to grow we somehow connected because I always spoke to him with truth and I felt it was better so that we can get through this life facing shit for what it is, like "I'm an angry bitch; don't get in my way!" He never speaks much because his insecurities make him hold back sometimes I have to pry out what he's feeling especially when he gets sad. Being a mom is a twenty four hour never ending job. Being a child is so much more fun, too bad I stopped when I left home at the age of fifteen; "Why for the life of me did I want to grow up again?"

Time has proven over and over the type of kid I ended up with was strictly because of me; yes we can blame the world and outside influences but the reality is what our children take from us determines who they want to be; yes; my son is a happy boy because I am the angry. He doesn't like me angry because he fears one day I'll really hurt somebody. I just happen to dislike people unlike him with many friends. He used to go to the congregation and love participating while I shriveled down in my seat; that boy loved the microphone I was so proud of him when he gave his first talk. I remember when he loved going out with the brothers of the congregation and going door to door to preach, meanwhile I stayed·home and drank beer, "Oh what a sin!" Who cares life is life. Every Sunday morning we'd go do our best to show up early at the congregation he loved to go; I just wanted a good seat. Again the good thing is that he's different then me because he doesn't know better yet.

Forever I've protected my son and fought most of his battles I don't know why it just comes natural sort of like animal instinct. I've resulted to giving his teachers attitude, and yes "I hate teachers." That's an easy one for me. Maybe I've wished a teacher ever place their hands on my kid that would be awesome if only once; that's a dream to me to kick a teacher's ass in her own class, wow! I could see it clearly my son embarrassed with me yet proud that I come to rescue, somehow he seems to like my defense track although he won't admit it. I've pushed and cursed little boys out; I played football with him and his friends I quartered back. If any one hurt him I yelled at them. I told one of his teachers that if he got hit by another student and he warned her prior, I totally agreed with self defense. I had no problem if a parent came to look for me. When you're a mother you truly feel huge like it's your place to do what ever it takes. At times I used to tell my son no one can hurt me, what a crock of shit but he apparently believes it because he's still scared of me.

My son once decided he'd not listen to rules anymore when he was sixteen, so I pushed him with threats of "go on, go and be a man into the world if you can you little punk!" So the outcome of months of that was he ran away to his friends house (Loser) that little "FAG ASS BITCH!" My son and loser became inseparable because apparently what they had in common was being raised by mom and no dad. I still hate him and his stupid mother who lied and said he wasn't there to the cops; lucky for her we don't run into each other and that's because I don't hang with losers. I knew in my gut though because I know my son to the T. So that was a Friday when I came home to a note and all my movies were gone along with some of this clothes his X-BOX, and god forbid he leave behind his NIKE collection but my movies, really. I wasn't going to let loser (A.K.A) punk ass fag, beat me with my child, so I was crying devastated and my friend Dean there by me comforting and making me not as depressed, but it was like my son took a sword from the living room and put it through me. What an awful revelation and to live it was worse. I wasn't about to let him leave me here alone without him he was my child, too bad he was angry with me so I followed my heart Monday afternoon and left work early because my son knew my schedule and as I drove past losers house well you can imagine my sons face when I rolled up next to him with the passenger window down and said "get the fuck in!" Yeah he couldn't be brave enough to ever run; I knew my son too well; and do you know what his loser friend did he left him and kept going not to deal with me. Again, "I win!"

My son is my monster the heartbreak of me and turning him in to a man is the most difficult shit I've had to do. It isn't easy you know because kids wear you down and you find that you're being too harsh and protective so he begs you to give him a better curfew and he won't try to run away again. "Now (ain't) that some shit!" He got me, now he's playing my game on me; I gave him props for trying to show me he can be tough and stick to his guns, but he also told me he didn't like it at losers and that's because hanging out at someone's house is not the same as living in loser Ville; my son only knows home. He took himself out of comfort Ville to realize homes not so bad. What a great lesson. "Being Mom is great! Being a child is not, ha-ha!" Again I win! If I could count the many tears I cry for my boy, if he only knew how hard being a parent is; kids are so stupid aren't they; I'm glad I'm grown up although I believe I was always mature since very young I mean I've been on my own since I was fifteen can't take that from me. Who would have thought that he'd be the inspiration for wanting to beat your kids without leaving a mark?

I actually stopped whipping my son with the belt on his hinny when he went to junior high because I told him we'd talk things out rather than to hit him for corrective action; but don't get it twisted if it was sever enough; "oh he'd get a smacking!" I am old school, kids should never disrespect parents. Besides all of the bad things we also had good and when I needed to talk out my feelings he'd listen and even sometimes give me a hug and a kiss; "Sorry babe: I know you're a push over even if you pretend to not be. So why do I hate kids? One great reason is my own kid, because man after all the sacrificing and struggle can you believe what he did? He forgot everything I ever taught him because he started hanging with loser again after his best friend GP died in a car accident. I believe he wasn't hanging with loser for some time but this apparently pulled him back in. "Don't you think it's exhausting already and don't you just hate fucken loser?" Depressed boys tend to find one another. For some reason this boy has a power over my son which makes him do very stupid things, like I understand getting high is fun and all but why must he come home at all hours of the late night and not go to college or keep a fucken job? All the two do is ride around in their stupid Hondas. Which by the way I spent tons of money paying for all of my sons car whims which I call "GARBAGE!"

I knew from the start that blue eyed five pound seven ounce crier was going to be hell I just never thought of how much hell I would get because my pregnancy went well. "How bad can it be, right?" When my son was little I liked buying him things whether it was because his father would disappoint him or lie to him or not pick him up or not send him money when he wanted something really bad, because with me he had to work for anything because nothing comes free. So I have always felt as a mother that my son resents me for leaving his father and I've spent these past nineteen years trying to make it up for god knows what. I mean it "I will never recommend children because CHILDREN JUST SUCK!" You don't get to breathe after kids "who's perfect plan was it to procreate? You owe me an explanation!" God forbid you do something nice for yourself. The one time I did something for me without involving my son, he got depressed started to cry and even threw in my face "This is the first time you ever left me alone!" Can you believe that little ingrate? I couldn't breathe anymore I needed space and time away from even him too. He was nineteen already and he only focused on me having two days out of nineteen years to myself. "Fucking incredible" that's what kids do they suck the life out of you and still they want more. Kids suck!

Chapter Four

To all the losers
of the world

It's so clear the memory that I still can't believe I actually saw the most beautiful thing turn ugly. It was behind the elementary school where my son attended, and it was me a friend, my son, and her son on the team. What a gorgeous hot summer day. My friend convinced me to go watch her son play on a baseball team, for moral support and my son was one of his closest friends, so without hesitation I decided that this time of the many

I was asked to attend, I'd go. For the record watching little boys play baseball isn't as fun as we think. No one tells them how much they suck because the parents pay to have them on a team; every parent thinks his or her child is the best of the team; these teamsters all whine, cry, pout throw the bat or helmet to the dugout area; basically the kids are to young for such harsh punishment from the pressure of thinking they have it in them to hit a home run, or catch that ball without dropping it; or even reaching first plate. It's like the parents want to live vicariously through their spoiled brat so they choose baseball and frankly if you watch closely the kids are all miserable until oh wait someone hit the ball by accident and the kids start to cheer for a few seconds or the child actually gets to first base. I believe that kids should not be allowed to play little league until they're 14 and can handle losing better.

There he was out of the blue, this little blonde blue eyed beauty, so beautiful that I was struck with amazement, I didn't watch the game anymore because my attentions were stuck on this little boy, at times I'd look over to see his mother cheering him on I actually believe he was one of the better players but I was too shell shocked to follow the game. In my head I was flabbergasted by this precious little boy with eyes clear piercing blue; he looked like a commercial child; the resemblance to his mother was none; I stood there thinking what a lucky mother it was obvious the child took after his father in every way. I secretly pretended that I was into the game for my friend but could care less I was shaken by flawless beauty. When the game ended I walked slowly to the car constantly looking back at this child and I couldn't for the life of me figure out why I was struck by his beautiful face. I mean I thought my child was precious but this boy had something about him. Little did I know at the time that it was a sign; maybe even a warning. Do you believe in destiny because I believe we see things beforehand just sometimes we can't put a finger on it; sort of like something's meant for you no matter how hard we fight it. Sometimes it's the awe striking beauty that we should all fear.

To all the losers of the world; I have this message for you. "He's mine, I made him; I love him; I will defend him and I will protect him from losers like you; you can't win a battle with a mother because you'll always lose whether sooner or later!" It started at sixteen, from tenth grade like a continuous cycle. Parents say they didn't see it coming when their child changes; but I saw my sons changes every step of the way. The beautiful child I once saw in a baseball field re-entered my life as now the new friend my son made in high school A.K.A. (loser). It's so incredible destiny isn't it; it's like a forewarning of a huge storm ready to come. My son introduces him to me still a beautiful child only older with eyes that pierce your heart like the devil enchanting temptation only I was now aware of the devil behind his eyes. I couldn't see it when he was a child but as a teen I saw my son wanting to be more like him; my son drawn by his charisma being a follower and not a leader automatically fell for this kid's bullshit on his take of life. The funny thing is that the devil is never ugly or mean; he comes in my house with his sweet smile saying "hello, Ms. Mendoza" and or "Have a good day." Too polite if you asked me, automatically I didn't trust him, trying to run game on me. Moms always follow their instinct because we know when the cradle is being rocked.

As a mom we have to allow our children to fall so that we're there to pick them up; and as messed up as that is for us it's actually our job and trust me that job sucks. Mom verses loser only means son hates you now mom. Every thing I ever taught my son goes down the tubes and when all else fails who do you think looks right in the end; yes that little fucker loser. I've learned not fighting it is winning it. I started to see my sons grades drop drastically; his teachers e-mailing complaints about my son disrupting classes, and although I think teachers suck; I had meetings with teachers and my son, I'd make him apologize to them before me and let him know that they could call me at any given time of day with a complaint with him present so that I could have a talking with him; this of course worked for a while but then it just got too damn annoying. He knew I'd eventually get tired of a teacher talking crap to me about my own little boy.

It started out with punishment which was no loser today, then no freaking X-BOX, to no computer; to no phone and it worked most of the time and the thing to learn here is that we mothers are such suckers for our kids; they learn you and trick you; they learn to lye through their teeth. "Did you stop hanging with loser?" "Yes, I did mom, I'm trying in school; it's just hard." "Okay then, stay after school and ask for help!" "I will." Kids are the devil, and frankly I don't care if I'm the only mother to speak out the truth. My son spent lots of time upsetting me and it became a constant crying for me while trying to work; I'd break down to my friend Dean who frankly in my eyes is the best person I know; who would of thought that a man with no children could help me get by, these situations. What situations; well kids in my home hanging out while I'm at work eating me out of everything I bought for the house, going through things that didn't belong to them nor my son; such disrespect for another persons house; and yes my son allowed it because he thought he was the man of the house because I spent my entire life telling him this was our home. I forgot that it was my home and my son was just a resident by obligation to me. Our home which he believed was his because I owed him everything for ruining his entire life; can you believe that one day the lady upstairs told me that his friends climbed through the windows even when my son wasn't home; too bad she told me after my son first ran away; it would have been helpful to know this information; but well at least she did tell me; so that I could prepare for the future.

When my son ran away to losers because he didn't want anymore rules I should have just never looked for him so maybe he could have ruined his life and then come back begging; but no as a parent we cry, we suffer; we nurture our baby; "what kind of bullshit is that dear God, I want to know." Yeah, because it's wrong to society if a mom doesn't care but caring is just pain and disappointment; I never want to know about kids ever again, because kids all suck. I had to care if my baby would graduate, so that his life could be possible; we seem to forget there are millions of people who don't graduate and still somehow survive. The thing is that we'd like to believe that our little boy is nothing like loser and can't understand the boys pull on my son; we wish something bad happens to loser, but God forbid. There were moments I believe that my son really did try to keep the peace between us; but he also slowly separated form me; we'd talk less, and I stopped talking to him because he now started talking hoodlum which I never understand that crap; and definitely don't respect anyone talking to me like "Hey ma, what's hood" fuck that I want respect from my son.

I never allowed him to wear pants down to his ass I sure wasn't going to allow him to talk to me like a hoodlum; "I'm his fucken mom!" Never in my day would I talk to my mom in that manner and I definitely made myself clear and yes I demanded an apology.

Now hanging with mom suddenly wasn't cool he even stopped kissing my cheek like I used to love; and I even tried to converse with him about everything that I felt as a mom to a son that had changed and change is good if for the better; I so hated loser with passion, the more he was involved with loser the more I started to view my son a loser as well. I actually asked "if he was gay?" Do you know why; because I couldn't see what could possibly make him love this kid so much without it being some sick twisted shit; It's a pretty lousy feeling to think to you as a mom "I'd rather he told me he's gay so that I can at least understand it better." Time just kept dragging and I felt like I was giving up so no more anger spieled out of me; I was restless, exhausted and I just didn't want anymore of it. There were moments when I could tell they weren't so close at times because my son would choose to spend time with me and other friends instead of loser, oh how I longed those days got longer and we'd actually have good days together and we'd shop and eat out for lunches or breakfasts and take a day in the city; and we'd have pleasant times; but he had withdraws and I knew it; because he'd sleep a lot; and usually that's a sign of depression one's I got no control of. I could deal with that and I'd try to make up for it by talking with him and letting him know that I was the one person who would understand and love him no matter what. But of course life has to fuck you; and ruin his now comfortable somewhat new found communication with his mom; because he's graduated and confused about life so he decides that after one month of college for which you paid for him to go after waiting a year of him taking a break from school, that it's not for him and you only found out because you trusted he was actually going; while all along he was hanging out with his new girlfriend while you were at work.

Oh, did I forget to mention I had to place cameras in my home because I couldn't now trust him because Mr. loser wasn't allowed on the premises after me coming home early one day and he locked himself in my bathroom leaving me no choice but to kick and scream at the door until I calmed and just allowed him to come out and I asked politely he never return. I guess my son resented me for distancing them too; but who the fuck cares. Let me just say on record "I love cameras; every mom should invest; trust me you will not regret it and when your childish brat tells you "where's the trust?" You make sure and say "you broke that trust when you thought this was your house and not mine!" I wanted so badly to regain the special connection we used to have; at this point I already knew that it was gone and no matter what I did I could not fix it. Loser probably thought it was great to ruin this (what used to be wonderful) relationship; what Loser never got is; in the end I always won; and yes it was thanks to him. "BRAVO mom!" Look at it this way; I may have fought constant battles; in which he felt he won; but the war wasn't over I beat my kid without leaving a mark you know how? Guess what happens to a child who lived his whole life with the one person who always made things alright for him. He misses you, and realizes one day, that no matter how many losers in the world exist and make fun times; there's only one mom and he lost her over stupid loser.

Yes I gave my son the choice of getting a job because yes he became a loser for not being able to keep a job for hanging with loser, or the option of joining the Navy because he'd threaten me that that's what he'd do, if he didn't get his way because he knew I didn't want him sent to Iraq ever. Kids try everything to hurt you intentionally when they are spoiled punks without a clue. "I fucken hate kids" that's right; I said it and I'll keep saying it because I have the right. Hell I don't even want grandchildren. One child was enough thank you. Well guess what I finally blew my top after going away for a few days in the city the one he tried to guilt me into not going, but I had cameras now fuck that; I needed a break from the world, so I can figure out what it was that

I wanted; "yeah what do I want?" "I want to not feel." That's what I want. Two days after I returned from the city I blew my top after work and I basically dragged him to the Navy Recruiting center in Bay shore New York and can you believe the recruiter told me I could not force him because he was of age; that's such bullshit; so I'm stuck with this little fuck. I was so angry I told him his options while we drove home from the recruiters office; I said "Boy, you better join on your own or get a job and start paying rent because you're not going to live off of me like some loser" I didn't take shit from his father I sure as hell wasn't about to take it from him.

I'd like to believe my son started going backwards when his friend GP died in a car crash and needed loser to help him have fun times. He never understood that sometimes you have to face life for what it is and what it is; is just life. He text me the next day that the Navy was out so I had to do what most mothers do when he decides to move out bringing the cops to harass me in my home while he took his clothes and sneaker collection because it's all he owned, everything else I ever bought him he sold because he was broke. He never valued that I worked hard to buy him everything I did; I was devastated. In the end you realize you create a monster for trying to protect your kid from all the horrible things like drugs, loser friends, no goal to achieve and that you can't fight their battles sometimes we have to set them free and learn it on their own so that they can see real life on their own; he learned quick sleeping in his car and having his real friend show up at my home to talk for him because he text me after leaving that <u>he hopes "I like dying alone</u>." Isn't that great! Stupendous! What he didn't know is that now when he wakes up he's still depressed because mommy no longer shows that she needs him, and that's because although I miss my once baby; He's now on his own to find out what kind of man he needs to be if he ever wants respect from me. He will never set foot in my home after what he's done to me the only person who had his back a million times more than loser. The way I see it is this "Fuck me once shame on you; fuck me twice go to hell." Through great connections I get to see all that he writes on his facebook page. He doesn't sound happy and feels alone; now he's even signed up for the army, who knows if it's true he's got a drug test the month of July.

Guess what loser; "If my son joins the army for three straight years, he's not coming back the same little boy. Guess what I won; my job is done;" I raised him to stand on his own and "now you will see he did this to come back to me; you stupid kid playing a game you don't know." You could never beat a mother, and that's how you beat a kid without leaving a mark the mark he feels is that he misses mom; "he's waking up and you're not fun anymore." This goes out to all the losers of the world. "For the record I hate kids."

Chapter Five

MEMORIES

Sometimes when I'm driving on a Sunday morning and I'm feeling a bit low because I miss my child; I say child when in fact he's grown is a sign that parents never want to let go and even though you hate on all kids at this point you still view them as child. I try to remember good things about the boy I once knew. Like how he had this perfect smile that he gave when he wanted to ask for something. He always knew how to tell you he loves you and suddenly out of the blue would say he loves you. I like talking good things about my son and not just the bad. I think every mom out there wants to be proud of her son. I truly did raise a good boy he just happened to lose his way for some time; but he's polite, quiet, and until he told me to "enjoy dying alone" never once disrespected me. I know he was angry, we all say angry hurtful words at some point of our lives. When I was young I had the option of not having my child; I could have done it but I guess I'm super glad I had him, because everything I have to remember is priceless to me.

When my baby monster was born for the couple of days we were in the hospital I remember being afraid. I was actually scared of everything that would happen once we left the hospital because he was so quiet and I loved his big blue eyes which turned to green then to hazel brown and his beautiful black hair fell off to turn blond to now brown. So many changes, and the changes were mine to be seen by, he'd hold my index finger for dear life and I would spend hours watching him sleep like suddenly my focus on life was quickly shifting and nothing and no one had meaning except for this little life. It's so great the precious moments that you have with this little monster. I don't care about anyone else I know I've done my best with my little creature. It may not have been perfect, and what a hell of a ride; but someday he'll be in those shoes; and say thanks to mom. Picture this if you will his first New Years I dressed him in a baby tuxedo slide into buttons on leggings he was so precious my everything this little monster who kept me up nights stood there looking angel and I love this picture of him, wouldn't you want to cry tears looking at your baby so cute. At that moment I could love no one more than him not even my mother. He was mine; all mine; I felt an empowering over him; like I made that and he's all mine. I resented his father and made clear of what were his rights; I was selfish about him and with him. It would be great if women could make babies all on there own wouldn't it. I'd shower him, and he loved water beating his head; we laughed like we had our secrets baby and mom, I'd sing and played it was like living childhood through another beings eyes; and my childhood sucked so to me this was great. I even wrote a song for him titled "This one's for you". Read Below:

This one's for you
By: Liz M. Mendoza

I feeling lost so all alone
Times had turned my heart into stone
Now with the changes that have come
Life is brought back by my own son

This one's for you, for the love in me you bring
For the me in you I see; for the kid I couldn't be
This one's for you, for the eyes that see for me
A second chance so differently, for the me in you I see
This one's for you; this one's for you, this one's for you

I'm not as perfect as you see
Try but mistakes are part of me
We we'll both learn as we both grown
I only want you to know

This one's for you, for the love in me you bring
For the me in you I see; for the kid I couldn't be
This one's for you, for the eyes that see for me
A second chance so differently, for the me in you I see
This one's for you; this one's for you, this one's for you

That is words from the heart of a mother; you can't make that shit up if you try.

Its funny how easily one forgets to mention the little things that matter, because we get caught up with being a parent who converts into responsibility first, and the child becomes a being just learning along the way with lack of guidance viewing parenting in a whole different light, from a totally different perspective. I think that having left home at such a young age made me such a different minded child, I forgot what being a child felt like because I hadn't been one for so long. I believe that it's important to try to remember that when we're going through so much with our children because trust me we can easily forget. I speak from experience. Kids are the life and death of you. We need to remember it sucks for both of you to co-exist. There are a million things to learn from kids; like remember when you had to walk your baby back to bed because he sleepwalks. I was always in fear that he'd walk out of the house. He fell out of bed constantly even if I placed him next to the wall he somehow found his way back and down to the floor. I heard my son cry sometimes at night; and I'd go by his side and caress him gently until he soothed to quiet. There were also the moments he came to my bed afraid of the dark. It's such a cruel thing we do to our children telling him the boogie man will get you, to teach them not to go there. Yet it comes out so naturally then we want to kick ourselves in the ass for putting fear into his brain. My son used to suck a pacifier until about two and a half and man was it difficult to wean him off; he'd literally go into the garbage and get it; I even dipped the pacifier into hot sauce and can you believe he loved his pacifier so much that when he sucked and got burned he still kept trying. He eventually forgot about it. I told him it got lost "Bullshit!"

To me personally the best years of mommy and child are between five and ten, because they are speaking in full complete sentences and acknowledge everything between good bad, respect order obey you still; don't try to question reasoning nor do they fight it. Teenagers suck, I mean truly suck we should be able to press a button where we can choose if we want to go through those years because I tell you every mother will have a loser to deal with; no exceptions " I call it three years or more depends on you of un-necessary bullshit." Oh the pain, thank god I am a woman of strong nature because if I wasn't he'd stomp all over me. I suggest a few things to parents, one definitely cameras screw trust; don't trust jack. Loyalty doesn't exist in teenage Ville. You know how they sell those waist or hand leashes for keeping your child safely by you, I suggest even though you may hate teachers today as well, cell phone, house phone, e-mail every kind of communication with each and every teacher and let your child know nothing will pass by you because they're on your personal leash. I tried the list of duties and rules on the refrigerator but that doesn't work they don't stand in front of refrigerators. Three, always make your schedule exactly opposite of seven to five; they learn you, this specifically if you're a single parent. Peer pressure can be a dangerously weakening factor for teenagers. Hence the excuse "but you don't understand." If I hear those words one more time, I will explode. What children forget is we are not enemy, and I really would like to know at what point your child likes you waking them up with a pillow smashed at his face to them forgetting that a day ago he placed his hands on your cheek out of the blue to say "I love you mom" to today being pissed texting his friends "I hate my mom." Really ouch that really hurt. The first time you read those words and yes you can pay a thirty dollar fee and get your child's cell phone texts even calls for the past year if he's on your plan. I was ready for anything thanks to loser friend. It's unfortunate, because after you feel hurt by your child something becomes damaged in you, and it's hard to re-coop but you have to by no choice, be strong. Again, "I hate kids." I love telling myself that, heck if children can hate on parents then why parents can't hate on kids.

One day my son will read this, as he should because he should know the way that I feel too, because what the immature ass doesn't recognize yet is that we were a team since day one, and I've fought hard for him to finally see how damn much I have loved him so much it hurts deep. I used to feel like he was my best friend until the whole loser era, that's unfortunately past and I really miss it, because it was the best of all time. My son so looks like me and I feel so proud that his face resembles mine I always have, it's like the mini me boy conversion. There are so many things to love about our kids, like his new hair style moments, when he no longer wanted me to cut his hair, and his "I can pick my clothes now" "wow, check him out" I thought, trying to become a man. What about "can I please have allowance for the things that I do". You think he's catching on, "go ahead boy, learn." What about when he surprises you with one of his friends cooking you dinner before you got home cause you're always exhausted from a long day. Granted they burned the stove top covers with the heated grills, and it may have been salty, but he did that for me. What about the moments he actually did what you asked and laundry was separated and the house was clean, he's a clean boy thank god because he likes order. When you found the garbage neatly by the curb and you didn't have to ask, or when he was proud of his report card and you'd take him out to eat where he wants for his accomplishments. I really miss those moments; those are the special memories to me. When he used to hold my hand when we walked in the mall not feeling shame because I was his mom; yeah you never get that back what a shame.

I remember the first time I taught my son to ride a bike, push, push and away. It's like standing back so proud he learned on his own then he falls "oh no, I let go too quick" I laughed but it's not funny he messed up his knee. It's there where I'm laughing but it doesn't seem cute; it really is "awe the memories." Somehow I consider those moments a parent's payback yet not intentional still it smells sweet. Imagine me and him in my car that I love, trying to teach him to drive, that was an explosion and almost cost me big time if he would have hit the neighbors car; it only took me one time and I got frustrated and said never again. Yup, I love him but ruin my car and it's on we will war. I don't have patience because I work a certain way with anything I do; like we couldn't wash dishes together it was always either him or me; do you know how many dishes and glasses my son has broken in life countless and I only found out by trial and error, or the lack of dishes I found to have; and forks it's like he'd throw way or lose them somehow; I could swear we had a ghost. The chores made for us where he cleaned the bathroom and I did everything else. He took out garbage and I picked up what overflowed, he separated laundry and I did the wash with and without him eventually.

My son was on a little league one summer because of course he wanted to be on a team like his friend but that didn't last, it was affecting congregation schedule. Besides truth be said he sucked. I'm not one of those parents who can't be truthful. Of course I lied and told him he's good, yeah but he was a crier and I had to go to the dugout and scold him for crying, telling him it's just a game. They used him as a bunter with that I say it all; his talent was running, sounds pathetic right? He tried out for school teams but never made the cut, then one day when finally he did; he was already friends with you know who. He did track for a bit but again he just quit he always blamed someone else for all his mistakes, this was his pattern. My son is Mr. excuses and it felt like pulling teeth when wanting facts from him, and he just shut down completely when not wanting to deal with things; I never understood that because he was my son how was it possible to be so different from me; quite the puzzle. I'm very expressive and open and honest with him and him totally the opposite with me. There are things in life that will have no explanation, "I feel so yipped!"

My son "I love you; through thick and thin, since day one to forever and death do us part. I miss you, and need you to co-exist, I am proud of you in all that you do, and yes you will make mistakes and have as well as I, but I promised you since you were a boy, I will make you a good man if it kills you. We are not apart we are living in this life and sometimes the ride is rougher than we think, so if you do the army thing and it's all the truth we will someday be better and stronger, I'll fail you not. I am your mother, your truest friend, your strength even when you don't see that; love is tough sometimes but it comes with purpose; I love you because you are my son and I would do it again if I had to as long as it's always you. Make me proud son because I will always, no matter what, without a doubt love you, I swear you that. You are my precious baby and no one loves you more than me, your mom." Forget loser friend.

This is the memory I want to give you so that it lasts forever engraved in your heart, because I know you have your own issues having been raised without your dad and if you need to blame me forever to be okay then do so, I still love you. You are the reason this book has been inspired and written because I love you so much, you should know that you are the life of me, my beautiful monster.

PS. "I still hate kids, smile for me."

Liz M. Mendoza

Chapter Six

ME AND YOU AGAINST THE WORLD

I always thought it was me and you against the world. Sure! Screw the whole proper you and I attitude, I say me and you because I was the stronger one in our relationship. I was Wonder Woman and you were like Robin Batman's sidekick because you were still young. But I always felt we were like partners, I wiped your tears and you would at times wipe mine and kiss my cheek to make me feel better when I was feeling low. We were supposed to not break that bond but by choice you did. I get it, but it just feels lousy when the world that I thought we had came to a halt. Heartbreaking is more like it; but why hold a grudge, I know you're going to grow up. The how to beat your kids without leaving a mark title came about me asking my friend Dean that question when you were sixteen and giving me so much bullshit stress while I'm trying to support us thinking about the future and you. For any parent who reads this book remember one thing about children, they don't come with instructions, nor are we perfect ourselves it's important to be honest with our children, about money, bills, loneliness and such. Show your imperfections but make clear your mistakes and don't promise things such as "yes, I will try to stop smoking, your right it's not good for my health." They throw that back in your face whenever you light up; just say "I'm addicted." Honest is good, you wouldn't want him lying when you ask if he's smoked pot, and drank at a party as a minor. This was where I did well; honesty is best policy. I tried to be as honest as possible. Do you know how hard the topic masturbation is with a boy; I don't know how long I was red and hot in the face for, but man it's hard. Yes single parents it does happen believe me, those long showers kill you at least it did me. Do you know what it is to be a very impatient being and waiting for a shower that only turns cold water once you're let in. I don't know how he did it but he figured out how to screw me. Imagine washing your hair under cold water jumping back and cursing your child out, "fuck, fucker, mother fuck!" JAIME!!!!!!!!!!!!!!!!!!!! My little brat lost his beauty pretty quick I'd say.

My son and me we're two and the same with some things, vanity was our best trait. Have you ever seen two women fighting for the mirror, the mirror in my home was tired of us we'd push each other out of the way while one wasn't done fixing themselves up yet. I understood me but my boy again, "mini me conversion to boy." Sometimes I actually had to get up from the sofa to ask him to get the hell out of the mirror 'because I saw his shadow on the wall thinking "what a jack ass." I can only imagine when he's a man, "sorry ladies it's all my fault." Wasn't intentional, it just happened to be. I was always telling him he was as beautiful as me because we came from beautiful people, "Yikes!"

"C'mon what's wrong with building your child's ego?" It's sort of like giving your child some money from child support when it arrived now that he was fourteen, not because I had to or that it was much but because this way he saw how much we received and saw that it wasn't a gold mine and mom isn't rich and could appreciated that I chose to give him a share. Eventually when he moved out I sent him the card through a friend, to help his struggle, but unfortunately by then he didn't appreciate shit, and thought it was owed to him, "do you believe that?" He actually had his pathetic father loser senior call me for the new card that would arrive because once he knew my son yes mine, was out of the house he tried to stop paying but the courts told him he was obligated until they say unless I closed the case on my own, what a dead beat. Now that's the dead beat of dead beats. I can't believe my son involved his father in our lives I wanted nothing to do with this asshole, who doesn't give a crap about (MY) son. The only reason I took his father to court for child support was cause he didn't even want to pay me twenty five dollars a week that I only requested not because I needed to depend on him but because milk was expensive when it came in a can. Somehow, unfortunately my son will need to learn to let go of the fairytale father he has imagined, and face the truth. I truly hope he never screws a child over, because it's just not right. Ladies listen good, don't allow your teenage daughters to spite you in anger, because they may end up with losers as this one, "I was young dumb and alone; "what's your excuse?"

Throughout my sons life I tried associating with my family in Connecticut, mostly the turnout wasn't pleasant and my son would see me cry on many drives back. His father used to pick my son up on some weekends when he lived in New York, but even that didn't go well, I had to go to a police station at some point because my son was always coming back hurt and I didn't trust what was going on fuck that, I went to him first and since talking didn't work I involved the police that's right if you can't protect your child from kids hurting him from your wife's side of the family, then I will, cause that's right "I DON"T GIVE A FUCK! It was good anyway because my son would come home with another tone and attitude that I got tire of rearranging. I never allowed my son to lose track of who he speaking to; again, "Old school till I die." Sometimes we try to influence our children with all good intentions but reality bites, and your family does suck no wonder my son is screwed up. I'm not saying that I'm not to blame for many things I take responsibility for all my actions and yeah we can all point a finger, but ultimately my sons best attributes are a reflection of me, he is who he decides to be. Just like I left my home at fifteen because I didn't feel like tolerating my mothers shit and knew I'd turn out better for walking away, the same goes for my son he knows life is full of choices and everything has a price; I have drilled that like a sledge hammer, if he hasn't gotten it yet, that makes him just dumb; and my son in everything but dumb.

My family member seems to think and for the record they're older than me I believe by three or four years, just can't remember exactly but they seem to think it's cool to smoke pot with their twenty something year old son, and brags to my son a confused being right now about who to look up to. Many people may feel different about this but I think it's wrong, just because when we're stupid teenagers experimenting with drugs doesn't mean that it's right, to try to be the cool grown up sharing a teenagers experimental drug sessions; it's actually very pathetic and make you my dear brother "a big time (LOSER) with a capitol L". "If you want to be a serious role model as one of the men that surround him, "you should grow up." I feel ashamed of my family and I'm one of them too, I drink and smoke cigarettes and I was never an angel, but my son is the main cause I chose the right path but at least work was always priority, before anything else because without responsibility how would I have survived raising him on my own. Even my son knows I can't count on family.

My son broke a team apart all for being head strong, maybe some of me was instilled only he chose the wrong battle to fight; I will never allow my son to choose to be a loser, because he isn't to me. He got a tattoo on his arm when he was eighteen because I wouldn't allow him until he became of age. Something to keep in mind parents, never say "you can do it when you're eighteen" because eighteen comes quick and they throw it in your face and you as a parent can't make promises to back out on them, at least I never did not with my son. So he got his tattoo and promised me not to get his ears pierced I asked him for his word and he gave me his word. The tattoo by the way talk about making a sucker out of me so he could keep getting more tattoos says "the love of women "Liz

Mendoza" "Was he slick or what? How can I not have like it; hell I was damn proud. On his other arm it had something with the name of GP. I guess that's how he promotes loving someone, I'm surprised, loser isn't up there, at least not yet that I know of. One never knows. After he left home though he came to my job to ask me for his car title because he was selling another one of his crappy shitty Hondas the car I will eternally hate, well I must say I was totally disappointed because the pain he wants to inflict purposely for his stupid mistakes, now more devastated to have notice he pierced both his ears, I've never like that look on men, now he's just like my brother with two ears pierced the other loser in his life.

Sometimes I feel I fought in life to survive, support, raise him, protect him and for what; kids are a bunch of ingrates, and in today's day and age have value for shit. If I would have raised him in the ghetto and had nothing to show, and for the record I have nothing to show I rent in someone else's home for the past sixteen years, because I like stability, I've had enough instability until I was fifteen, so I gave my son a normal environment, so shit like this wouldn't have happened yet loser made sure to rock that boat, he was probably envious of it. If we lived in the ghetto he might have appreciated everything instead of expecting, maybe or maybe not, I'll never know. As for all the crappy pieces of junk Hondas in which he made me invest in. That will remain the official car that I'm sure I'll never own. First it was the hatchback he begged me to buy so that he could invest his own money to fix, well it cost me three hundred, "hey he was sixteen" he wasn't getting anything new and no one ever bought me a car, so it was a gift, well he did nothing but dream while sitting in the car turning it on until it ran out of gas, a year no investing I made him have it junked, did he pay me what he earned for junking it? "No!" Then along came (Honda Paseo) a piece of junk that cost me not only the fifteen hundred I gave him to open and save in an account as part of his graduating present along with the HD PlayStation, and HP computer, plus printer/copier/scanner. All the money came from me and he emptied the account on this scrap metal junk that leaked from the shitty roof top window. Oh yeah I spent about twelve hundred plus, to make it useable, then another four hundred on a (Honda Prelude) that came with no title which he could never get because he was conned another junking of the car took place, did I see any money "hell no!" This all happened in the same year mind you just months apart; then finally his blue (Honda Paseo) the first one was white; in which it cost me eleven hundred because he broke the front end popping the clutch; incredible, right? A day later while driving he busted a rod. I really can't make this shit up right? "Thanks Pete for not charging me twice!" Wouldn't you hate your kid by this point? I kept giving him chances all he did was break me financially "hell I'm actually relieved right now by this point that he left." No it's still not over; I come home one day and the engine of his car is leaking oil all over the drive way because he and his jack ass mechanic want to be friends feel they had the right to take apart the engine I've just spent eleven hundred dollars on. It had a huge hole in it. "Are you fucking kidding me?"

"It was supposed to be me and you against the world" Well that shipped has sailed Robin seems to be trying to tear down Wonder Woman's defenses and that shit just (ain't) going to happen. Through trial and error I've learned you just can't keep saving someone; you have to (Listen real good, mothers) let your children fall and break their teeth because if they don't they'll keep leaving you broke and never once caring that your getting older; and I can't for the life of me see him taking care of me, "(Ain't) that some shit!" I love my son but I will never recommend children to absolutely anyone, it's a big "NOOOOO!" The process is a journey and yet, so fucken useless trying to get out of the relationship what we won't find; that's right he'll grow up but only because he has to because for him I no longer fight. Do you know what you learn when you live alone; that peace feels so good, and someone slamming the door every twenty minutes is finally over, and that you actually save money instead of being drained, and a son borrowing money without having any was a lucky bastard, because I'm a good mom. I also learned that being told to "enjoy dying alone." Really it isn't a bad thing. We were born alone and we do die alone "don't give me that twin shit, they come out one at a time". Plus we were born to die, "or is there some kind of medical break through that I know nothing about?"

Until my son is ready to be with me against the world, he will have to grow up some. Loser friend and I don't exist as two people in his life because he chooses loser so mom won't exist, because if he thinks that boy is going to be in my life by force he is so dead wrong I could give a rats ass if that boy died right now; "I have to wonder who's side God is on at times; I try not to but man; the question just rolls in my brain. And for the people who think they can make comment about me not caring or appreciating what my son has done for me "GO TO HELL!!! What do you know about my relationship with my son; look at your life with your kids before you spit up! FYI: "Gee, no one's heard from Liz. "I wonder why?" I hope I did my son justice by keeping it real because he knows what I write in this book is all the truth, about people we both know. The world is big, life is long, "but my dear monster baby boy, I will always await you." C'mon Wonder Woman's getting old and "I still love you, no matter what." "Still I have to say it, I fucken hate children!"

Chapter Seven

HAPPINESS IS ALWAYS
IN THE BOTTLE

I've always found pleasure in drinking. Some people do yoga, some get depressed, some do paraphernalia others look for lovers; etc. etc. Get the picture? My son's friend once told me in conversation "my son drinks like a pro." I was shocked because I knew he told me he has drunk before but like a pro really? He's never drunk in front of me because I told him I didn't agree to it and he would not disrespect me; again the (hypocrisy of motherhood) because I've been drinking since before I was fifteen thanks to lousy role models and family members the everything's I want nothing to be like. Yeah I am a firm believer of do as you're told and not what I do. I don't care that it's wrong it's my home my rules that's it my way or highway, fuck teachers with stress bullshit; mothers are in the stressed pull your hair out type of ready for heart attack situations. We deserve a drink because <u>happiness is always in the bottle</u>. If it wasn't for liquor there would be a lot more dead children in this world, "please go buy a bottle and make yourself happy because you deserve a drink, Salud ladies!"

I have never gone wrong with making myself feel numb because it's always good to not feel pain, and I understand that not every one handles liquor coma the same some people get angry, some get depressed but lucky for my strong spirits, I'm a happy drinker and I can occasionally grow beer muscles if someone messes with mine, naturally a protector. But being told my son drinks like a pro is more than shocking I mean how can a nineteen year old be a pro compared to a woman who had over twenty five years of practice really? Stunned isn't even big enough a word to handle such shock; "my man!" I'd like to say I'm disgusted but I'm proud "you go boy!" the only problem is he can't keep a job. Doesn't seem like a pro at all just a fool wasting his pathetic teenage life because happiness is always in the bottle if you can afford it. What ever happened to having a game plan? If you can't afford your choice of drug then why do drugs what's the point, at least go in hard with some sort of game plan because you can't really stake the title "Pro Drinker" and be broke as shit living day to day without respect from the woman who created you who's home you chose to leave for the party lifestyle you can't afford anymore. At least back in my day when I hung rough, and this isn't to brag but to make point, "I paid for my shit!" Not only that; but worked supported you made sure you had a safe and stable good home. Maybe that's the problem I should have not tried protecting you to the point where you were clueless to everything real. I had real in my life and I walked away, maybe I was just trying to keep my son safe; it suffocated him to feel so loved; what a shame. So this is where you end up for trying, hum! What a dilemma, so there is no such thing as a perfect mom I know, but you know what; there is no perfect child either "fuck that we go down together;" "Have another drink!" As, for looking for joy deep in the bottle you're drinking for the wrong reason; it's supposed to be fun, I drink to be happy because apparently I play well with the bottle and the bottle knows me and how much it takes to make me happy and do you know why that is, because in general I'm a happy being. "I LOVE to laugh."

Happiness is always in the bottle, for those of you who can compose yourselves properly because you don't have to be so dramatic. The problem with society is that it's overly judgmental; yeah everyone has an opinion, everyone has something to say or critique you about and incase you didn't notice everyone is FULL OF SHIT! The world is a bunch of hypocrites from children to mothers to fathers, to sons and daughters to cousins, aunts uncles and oh yes, even grandparents. Haven't you heard the one about your cousin giving head in a truck, but oh yeah it's okay for her to say "she's a drunk"; or how your mother was a cheating whore back in the day; wait I think my aunt spilled that one; or how one of your aunts beat her husband every time she drank. Or how your aunt thinks you screw her man behind her back. I mean really what a bunch of hypocrites. Hell if I didn't find happiness in the bottle I might have murdered someone by now. "I am not perfect, big fucken deal!" At least I know that everything that I have done to protect my son in life and raise him to become a good man has been done with good intention and he knows how very little I respect my family; yes I have been honest with my son that's right. It's up to him now to decide which way he wants his life to go, I already lived my life the hard way and frankly what anyone has to say about me I could care less. Happiness is always in the bottle because the lord knows it's not in family structure. One day my child, my ingrate bastard my love of my life will learn that it wasn't so bad, and you know what he'll probably view me as cool because I was and have been honest with him and that's what's important. Maybe I couldn't be fun but I gave him real and there is something to be said for that. "I always keep it real and say what others know to be true but don't have the "COJONES" to say because what? Everyone is full of shit!

If my son is pro at drinking then you know what? All I have to say is get a job and support your habit; don't drink and drive because that's a mistake trust me; and make sure you have a safe driver for those drunken moments. I've lived a long life and it's taught me many a lessons. I learned that maybe you can please some people but you'll never please everyone, and maybe you can't please anyone but who really gives a fuck; I mean who's the one placing the carton of milk on your table; is it really your gossiping family or friends or is it you, with your money, your job, or jobs as a matter of fact. I've learned that while you rise to the occasion people love to see you fall because they're envious that you make it on your own. So I want my son to rise to the occasion because those people he includes in his life right now talk shit behind his back only he's to young and naïve to recognize that I can't protect him any more, he's got to learn to fall and break a tooth every once in a while to realize who's burning him in his life; that's a mothers job; "doesn't that suck? A thankless job, I say." Don't you just want to hate children with me? "C'mon moms, you know you agree!" I learned recently that, that once quiet little baby in the hospital room was the greatest lesson for me. Yes, because it proves the strength a mother carries, and I am proud of myself. I often wondered why my mom cared more about her lovers than her kids, and for the record if she cared about her kids more it really didn't show, and yes I can say it because "I don't give a fuck it is the truth." I curse a lot, but hey whatever. Truth is I talk like a trucker or so I've been told. God I like honest people.

The only advice really that I have left for my son is "be happy; find what makes you happy." If happiness is always in the bottle then "I'm not one to step in your way and you know that." I've always told my son "do whatever you want because life is long and if you get tired of something, then try something else." I've done so many things thinking it's what I wanted at certain points of my life to figure out that I was actually happy with my profession all along. I work hard and I love that I respect my profession. I raised my son in this profession and I don't need to complain about being unhappy with my life because I absolutely feel great and I hope that my son finds what he likes for his life. People have a tendency of living regret for whatever reasons but I look at every piece of my adventurous life lived and think "wow, the pages to my life's book are incredible; aren't they? Fucken (A)!" Sometimes I feel like my middle name which was also my grandmothers (Modesta) meaning modest had to be mine because my life has been special and God gave me what I can bare; a little bit of everything. Happiness is always in the bottle because the bottle is always half full for me.

If drinking is all you do, and you don't beat your kids, and you work hard and like yourself at the end of the day then really you're okay. I look in the mirror and smile every time; and frankly I miss pushing my son out of the way "those were good times, good times." My son is a beautiful young man on his way in life and even though because of him I hate children, I love him so much. So to my son "Maybe some day when you are older and legally of age, you and I can have a drink together and reminisce the good old days of you and I." No one knows our package deal and frankly no one should because "I know our bond is priceless, it's just called motherhood."

Truth be said I'm really not jolted or scorned for all of my sons actions; I'm just saddened by his reactions to all the things I tried to do for him because while having loser friend in his life meant more to him than facing the truth from me. I understand children will do these type of things, but really "Enjoy dying alone; now was that necessary?" He already knew I was a loner; and that I have the attitude "you live to die, and you're born alone you die alone" I often wonder how he feels, because I know he has conscience, and that's not a good place to be so "If you find happiness isn't in the bottle anymore;

remember that I always forgive you, no matter what. That's the difference between loser friend's mom and him and you and I is we actually have a good relationship; you just push away." Happiness is always in the bottle because I will always have good words for my son; I mean what kind of mother would I be; if I allowed him to keep hurting me; the process of him joining the service is so he can see life for what it is and if it takes him three more years to learn then that is fine with me.

"Hey loser friend, mama always wins and one day I will toast with my son all about you." This is to all the losers of the world, "Salud!"

Chapter Eight

How to beat your kids without leaving a mark

What an interesting concept, how to beat your kids without leaving a mark, truth is you want to leave a mark don't you? It's our soul purpose as parents to make sure the bruise of life sticks. On the other hand wouldn't it be great to be able to beat your kids and not leave marks; that's a parents dream now a days since discipline is now considered abuse; "what a crock of shit." I remember a time when the school principle had a wooden board for disciplining bad students. Where a school teacher could wash your mouth with soap if you used bad language in class; "yeah those were the good old days;" kids used to respect teachers, and fear the wooden board. A bad kid stood out in class and no one ever wanted to be the one facing the chalk board in front of the whole class, or step outside the class room for about fifteen minutes; in fear that the principle would walk by and question what one did. The good ole days; when cleaning the chalk board erasers outside were a privilege and not a shame. I'm glad I used to get whipped by my mother for doing bad things, maybe she was aggressive at times but I got the point didn't I. My sole purpose of this book was to vent; and venting is good, again some people use other methods of venting like drugs, lovers, etc. I choose to let it out and to be honest it's been good for me always; so this is where it is the story of how to beat your kids without leaving a mark. What a great title I say all stemming from me asking my friend that question one day while frustrated with my son, and he said "You should write a book with that title everyone would buy it." I doubt that but still after the whole "enjoy dying alone" faze I told myself "you know what; maybe I will."

Truth is I have no regret for not allowing my son back into my home until he fixes his life because frankly I taught him better and if he wants to behave like a loser well then he knows I don't hang with losers; I used to but not since I've grown, that was a long time ago. Ask me how many people know my number and I can count with one hand. I do believe you can beat your kids and not leave a mark; but someone will have to be the test monkey for my theory to be proven. I think if you took a book holding it to your child's behind and spanked the child really hard "oh you beat him and amazing; no marks." Again but that's up to the parent willing to try; it's just an idea. I've always liked to think of myself as someone who likes to think out of the box. Being that I was and still am a person who faces things and life for what it was and is I think this book is just one of those things I had to do; sort of like not allowing my son to weasel his way back into my home after all that he did; a partnership consists of two people and not one always being left high to dry. When people decide to have children it's to procreate life and through the process one becomes at least most of the time structured responsible and very weak at the same time; if the world was run by children imagine that how messed up it would be. We'd have skinny jean, pants off the ass, selfish, ignorant, all I know is texting, lazy and I mean very lazy children running the show; "oh no!"

Would a child think of the title to this book; most likely not they would probably pick a title instead of "how to beat your kids without leaving a mark" say maybe "why I need my cell phone, mom" or "got to have it; kick, kick and scream" or maybe "I hope you enjoy dying alone".

"Good one isn't it?" These senses behind writing this book was specifically an inspiration by my son and for all parents of the world please excuse my vulgarity, but I write like I speak; don't mean to be so vulgar I just am. I hope the message is clear for all those parents that still think they are obligated to take crap from their children. If they are over eighteen and smooching off of you and not working and coming in at three or four in the morning and not going to school or joining the military my true heartfelt suggestion is give them their options or out the fucken door. I found out recently that yes we have the right to not take them back in; they are of age. Trust me tears will follow and they'll have friends because yes these little fucks stick together like an alliance comes talk to you about how your son lives in a car and even a friends mother will get involved and beg of you to come over while your son is there so we can all talk civilly; "Are you fucking kidding me?" "What's all the shoulder rubbing for; my sons not dead." Say it after me women; "I will not be beat by the system; I choose my way or the high way." Hell I left my home when I was fifteen do you really believe I'm an individual that takes crap from anyone; really.

The purpose of this book is to unite all mothers and spread the word because this generation blows. I refuse to fall into it; because like anything else; imagine what the future holds. Can you imagine being old and these idiots run the old folk home you're in; what a disaster. I remember a time when absolutely nothing came free; and I liked it because it made me a better me. After this book I feel I can die now; you know why because my purpose is said and done. How to beat your kids without leaving a mark is my mark, and history in the making not bad for a Puerto Rican girl who left home at fifteen and maybe it's too short and maybe not close enough to becoming magnificent but man, while I sat here writing everything that is in this short story I felt good and invigorated to have fought back; round nine and I am still standing; how about that people. Words of advice for all the grown ups trying to be young again "face that it's not your place to relive youth" we don't grow backwards so stop trying to be best buddy with your kids it makes us real parents look un-cool and for the record no real mature parent thinks you look good, they just smile and talk about you; "go back to old school." That look doesn't make you cool just stupid. Plus your kid still runs game on you, fool.

Since the departure of my child from my home I realized I re-arranged some things like how I live; now I actually feel free of burden. Now I actually sleep better; now I have less worries; now the food in the fridge is what I want. Now after nineteen years of not existing it's all about me finally. How to beat your kids without leaving a mark was destiny. It seems my life had to happen the way it had for this book to be possible; "Every mom should write their own story." It's so relieving and stress removing; "God I feel good." If I didn't leave a mark; I at least left something and that's the story about how to beat your kids without leaving a mark. I wish there was a place sort of like jail but for teenagers that every time a parent got pissed off with their child could take them there for a day but not like a juvenile institution but more like a place where no electronics exist and they're stripped of communication from the world even they're parents and they have separate rooms where they have to do physical labor for a whole day and it has to be hard. Like placing a teenage boy on the bus and taking him to the tobacco fields for a complete day like back in the day when people took a bus like that and worked on the fields in the beaming hot ass sun; just see what would happen I bet he'd behave after that if you as a parent could used that threat; or a teenage girl scrubbing toilets in a women's prison facilities have you ever wondered how bad it gets the stench, and the disgusting bowl movement still in the bowl afloat having to plunge and make the bowl properly flush; I bet after a day doing that she'd come back ready for rules; don't you think? Yeah I do like to think out the box and give off the things that really suck in life because having no cell phone; isn't the end of the world and X-BOX or PlayStation is not what kids need it's a privilege granted by parents and the struggle they have to make kids happy.

Someone should really go up to the podium on parent teacher night and stand up for the parents; we aren't wrong; we are their teacher; and in today's generation sorry but "yeah; most teachers suck." How can we allow twenty something year olds most likely without children of their own leaving impression on our children and all high school teachers should meet a requirement to have kids that have been raised plus bratty grandkids before they can step on school grounds; the twenties to me are just too young to be teaching teenagers. On one of the parent teacher nights I had with my sons computer class teacher all he did was brag about his education and knowledge and the possibly of what kids could take from that course; I was nauseated and couldn't believe this young punk; really. I felt like walking out right there and then. The word possibly just doesn't sound right. "It should be definitely, to me." But what do I know I'm just a parent. "Where's the god damn sign up list for kicking a teachers ass;" I want to know. For all of you that may have come across my book and feel disgusted and appalled; well too bad; obviously it means we real parents don't hang with people of your sort. We actually care if our kids succeed in life. Enjoy your grand life.

For the record many who read this book may think I'm an angry woman, and I'm not really I just don't like this generation of children, or teachers for that matter. Also if I was angry then also I do have the right to be because thanks to my child I'm writing this book; and the intent is to inform the world of good parents to not feel the blame is on them because our children screw up and do selfish things, without a care in the world. If your child is between the ages of nine to thirteen and owns a cell phone, then shame on you. Do kids really need communication at that age or do you just want them to feel cool. My son at age fourteen had a cell phone because at the time he did have a job and paid for it himself. All the phones bought for him I broke or drowned because enough was enough. It felt good too; I won't lie; there's something empowering about breaking that stupid communication device; what happened to the era where people actually talked and made sense instead of the bull crap texted today and we are all guilty ourselves too. Also for the record the more tech savvy a child gets through time the less a parent really knows, go figure that one. What do your kids know how to do on Face book and websites that you know nothing of, and what garbage and idiotic things are they actually speaking. By the time parents figure if ever this information your child has all their information on many sites where people can view such things. Thank god I didn't have a girl cause I'd have to tie her up and keep her in the basement sort of way. "Have I mentioned I hate children?"

Read below and see how I beat my kid without leaving a mark.

6/27/10

Ma,

It's been a while since you've kicked me
out. I've been through alot and feel that
I have changed for the worse. I don't
know who I am or like who I've become
for that matter. I never meant to hurt you
because you are all I ever had in this
world, and I've lost that. I never even
wanted to involve my father but when I
was gonna sign up for the navy I needed
to pay tickets off but instead of him
sending me money he sent me a plane
ticket. I was there for 2 months and
regret it. for all the things I've said to
you I didn't mean I was just mad.
yesterday you turned 40 and your only
getting older. I wanna be there to care
for you as you get older because I
wanna be that man you raised me
to be. I did something for my own
good and signed up for the army

so I could get away and fix my life and
start a career for myself. Once I leave
for the army I will never associate with
Cody or his family. I don't wanna be
looked at as a loser as he is. Hopefully
my decision for the army is a good
one in your eyes because I wanna
be back on your team. From here on
I will turn over a new leaf so you
could be like "wow that's my son"
and be proud saying it. I've made
numerous stupid mistakes but I've realized
I will always need you and your guidance.
I hope your doing well because I LOVE you
and always will. July 6th I got to go
and see my recruiter for a drug test and
from that day that's when I sign the
papers saying im fully enlisted. That day
I will find out the actual day I leave
and I will let you know because I would
like to see you before I go if you want
to. As always I love you
    Good Bye   →

P.S. I am staying at alex's for
the meanwhile

From: Jaime

To: Liz

Chapter Nine

PARTING WORDS
FROM MOM

Well I'm feeling good about myself for speaking my mind on paper. These parting words from mom are my final. I don't have the answers nor the tricks to be slicker than kids; what I do have is my experience and hope it's used for the best outcome of dealing with your kids; oh and really "I hate all kids". I enjoy saying that it makes me smile. After nineteen years of saying I love you I now feel owed. (Ain't) that's right (Ain't) that some shit. I love my son dearly and one day he'll read this book and think "damn ma, you're fucked up" and I'll say "uh, huh!" So maybe I may not have made miracles in this life; or won lotto to boot; and maybe I'll never be famous for writing this and such but that's definitely not why I do this; I do it because knowledge is good, experience is better and kids will always suck. Doesn't matter the generation, but imagine the future generations, God help you parents.

If I had a nickel for every time I said kids suck; I'd probably be very well off. My parting words from mom may not seem positive nor great words, at that; at least I keep it real; because kids really do suck. For women planning on having children don't go out and buy those cute how to parent guides cause that's just a total rip off; if you feel the need to spend money for the heck of it; heck send it to me and maybe I'll start a foundation for one of those bad child working schools and name it (The institute of Workforce KS), short for Kids Suck, Founder and CEO Liz M. Mendoza. How many mothers wouldn't love to partake in such a good cause? I know you're out there, lets go covert and make time for a meeting I need some real mom soldiers and yeah you can wear the whole tactical clothing "cause and affect" I say. "Where are all the real moms?" Classes available:

Class Schedule:

(Classes Not Optional/Recommendations Only Need Parental Consent).

1. TF Unit 5am -5:00pm Foot Note: (TF stands for Tobacco Field)

2. PQP Unit 6:30am – 6:30pm (F) Foot Note: (PQP stands for Prison Quarters Plumbing)

3. BLWC Unit 7am-7pm (M) Foot Note: (BLWC stands for Brick-Layer Wall Construction)

4. STC Unit 8am-8pm (M/F) Foot Note: (STC stands for Shark Tank Cleaning) and yes they will be in a cage. "Don't worry; Liz will take care of it."

5. BV Unit 9am-9pm (M/F) Foot Note: (BV stands for Burn Victims)

6. AMI Unit 10am-10pm (M/F) Foot Note: (AMI stands for Army Medical Infantry)

Do you get the message, "They will." We aren't giving them no cheesy classes like Cosmetology or home economics; fuck that let them do real ass jobs, and see if they like scrubbing the skin off a burn victim or calming down a soldier with a blown leg or something. Again, "cause and affect."

Sign up sheets available at www institute of Workforce KS.

Best Regards,
Liz M. Mendoza

Parting words from mom. "I love my son but I hate kids!"